I0212476

PLAY NICE.

The Journey of Parenting, Co-Parenting and Life In Between

Deirdre Bey

Deirdre Bey. © 2019

All rights reserved. No part of this book may be reproduced, stored, or transmitted by any means- whether auditory, graphic, mechanical, or electronic- without written permission of both publisher and author, except in the case of brief excerpts used in critical articles and certain other noncommercial uses permitted by copyright law. Unauthorized reproduction of any part of this work is illegal and is punishable by law.

ISBN: 978-0-578-49331-2
Editors: P31 Publishing, LLC

Because of the dynamic nature of the internet, any web addresses or links contained in this book may have changed since publication and may no longer be valid. The views expressed in this work are solely those of the author and do not necessarily reflect the views of the publisher, and the publisher disclaims any responsibility for them.

Printed in the United States of America

Dedication

I dedicate this book to my parents, James and Patricia Tucker. Without your nurturing, love, guidance, and life lessons that you made look effortless, I would not have the knowledge to pass them on to my daughter, and your granddaughter Taí.

To my daughter, Taí, I've watched you navigate through this thing called life. While things were not always easy, you handled them as well as you could and continue to make me proud of the young lady you've become, always striving to live your best life.

To my husband, W.C. Bey. Thank you for your unconditional support and always being my biggest cheerleader. It takes a special man to come into a situation and not only accept me, but my child as well. You are that man and you have shown us love, patience and respect.

Finally, to my friends and family who always provide a healthy dose of love and support. To my OLG's (old lady gang), who have always been there to listen, laugh and cry with me through our most difficult moments of raising our daughters.

Table of Contents

Acknowledgements

To my daughter and all daughters, know you are always the prize. Love yourselves first and always.

To my brother James M. Tucker, who always encourages me and lets me boggle his brain with the phrase, "create the memories". Thanks for having a heart of gold and all of your support.

To all my ride or dies, since day one and beyond, you know who you are. To all my friends who are moms, show others how to love you through how you love yourself.

To Butch, documenting this journey has been 10 years in the making. I have always wanted us to get this co-parenting journey "right". This book started out as an idea about the relationship between our daughter and you, called *Letters to My Daughter* when she was in middle school. It became so much more because of you and others who have influenced me along the way. Finally to all the men who have crossed my path and shown me love and kindness, thank you for the examples of how you love yourself, your daughters, and others.

I thank everyone who has touched my life and made me strive to be a better me.

INTRODUCTION

There are countless studies that report when a daughter has a difficult relationship or the absence of a relationship with her dad it will affect other areas of your daughter's life. This affects her self confidence, self-esteem, relationships, trust, vulnerability, and she may also experience feelings of abandonment. I will go one step further and say these unhealed areas can cause a sense of psychological trauma. When dealing with areas where dad is in and out or unavailable, young ladies may exhibit signs of distress, which can also make them vulnerable. These points in their life can go unattended or unnoticed, because they are not aware of the root cause of their sadness, depression, or why they may have difficult relationships. This is my journey of parenting, co-parenting and everything else in between while raising a daughter to love herself, live in her truth and know her value. Single moms you may feel alone, but you are not. You must rely on your faith, friends, healing from within and taking care of yourself.

Whatever the circumstances surrounding a father's absence or intermittent presence he may have in his daughter's life, the impact is critical to the daughter-father relationship. The "why" may vary with each dad such as he has made a personal choice not to be involved, could be because of substance abuse issues, mental health issues, employment issues, divorce or just life events. In any case, his involvement or lack thereof, helps shape his daughter's emotional and mental health landscape.

My parents were married over forty years. I got to see and experience a father's love and commitment to his family on a daily basis. This gave me a sense of safety, a sense of belonging, protection, and love, which is what I hoped for when I had a child.

As it relates to my daughter's father, his rearing was a little different and as a result, he will say he unconsciously brought what he experienced with his mother to the relationship with our daughter. He will say he didn't know how to be in a relationship. He saw his parents co-exist separately. He never saw couples or marriages working things out or making long term plans. He never attended a wedding until his adult years. In the examples he saw, once something went wrong with one person in the relationship, you leave or move onto the next person. He said he never witnessed a healthy relationship during his childhood. As a result of his life experiences as a child and trying to find ways to cope, he later, turned to drugs, experienced mental health issues and struggled to manage life issues in general which played a pivotal role for him in his growth, development and parenting.

It has been my experience that men who grow up with nurturing moms tend to be more sensitive and attentive in their romantic relationships. They have core-values, like reverence, discipline and learn to value women early in their life. How a man deals with or cares for his "lady" can be a reflection of the type of bond he has with his mother.

On the other hand, and in the case of my daughter's father (whom we will call Butch), men who *are not* connected or have an unresolved bond with their birth mom, can be a little more complicated and fearful of commitment. For my daughter's father and so many other men who have the same experiences, they navigate through life a little different (their lenses are different). They may be involved in various relationships at the same time, cheat, and operate in the abandoned state of mind which often translates to them asking themselves the same question over and over again, "How can you love me and want me, if my own mother did not love and want me"? Sometimes unbeknownst to them, they get stuck in patterns of inner pain and shame. By his own admission, Butch found ways to push me and others away. Of course, this is not always the case with all men and with new efforts, new learning, and healthy relationship goals, it can certainty be different.

Again, this was our experience. Looking back we never really connected the dots until later on and having many conversations over our thirty years of friendship. I give you the background because in Butch's words, becoming a parent to a daughter only exacerbated the issues.

You've probably heard that having a strong male influence is important to a young man's life, but it's equally important for a daughter as well. A father does not have to live in the home to be a good dad. A father doesn't have to be perfect, but if he puts forth effort and shows commitment in his daughter's life, the rewards are immeasurable. This was the case with Butch. He gave what he had, and I was determined to bridge the gap.

When there are healthy interactions between a dad and his daughter, it helps create a positive self-image. It provides a secure base from which the daughter learns to explore the world and interact with others. When there is little to no bond between the two, daughters may be prone to depression, anxiety and her overall physical, psychological and social health can be affected. The long-term effects may be fear of intimacy, fear of commitment, issues of trust or struggles within her own intimate relationships. Children come into the world like sponges absorbing all we have; the good, the bad and the "where did that come from" and blame it on the other side of the (DNA).

You may ask why does this matter? Because for a daughter it's the first relationship she has with a man thus teaching her how she should be treated. He shows her how to "be". At different times growing up, these were my daughter's experiences. She felt abandoned by his actions, which showed up in her grades, her choice of friends and getting into unhealthy relationships.

Sometimes as parents we can fall short. Thankfully, God's grace and mercy can fill in our lack by putting people in our lives who can support and guide us, provide information, and help us rely on our intuition or internal voice to guide us along. You don't have to live together to be a good parent, just have the willingness and commitment to do so.

Chapter 1

~

My Family Looks Different: Re-Define The Reality

I first met Butch while working at the same non-profit organization, shortly after graduating from college. We dated briefly, then Butch got a new job closer to his hometown and we both moved on. After several years apart, we found ourselves together once again. We reunited during a time when both of us had changes with our jobs, and were subsequently working in the same area. As our relationship progressed, Butch and I decided to move in together. During this time, I found out I was pregnant. We became engaged and planned to get married. Our daughter Taí was born the summer of 1993.

It was 1994, a few days before Mother's day. One bright, sunny Saturday morning I was on my way to the hair salon and I left my Taí sleeping on her dad's chest on the couch.

This particular day I took Butch's car, instead of mine. I reached over into the glove compartment to get some lotion. Instead, what I found was a picture of a woman sitting on Butch's lap. I looked closer, although I didn't know her, I felt like I had seen her before. My heart stopped, I wasn't even out the apartment complex; I asked myself, do I turn around? Do I confront him? What should I do?

I went back in my mind, and said to myself, mm-hmm she's the same woman from the bowling alley a few weeks prior. I consciously filed her in my "alrighty then" file (a file in my memory, when something doesn't feel quite right. A group of thoughts I access anytime when needed and more importantly, when absolutely necessary) which I will discuss later.

Let me add, I talk with God on a daily basis. It has always been my belief, if I am feeling unsettled about something or need to make a decision, I ask God for guidance. If it's something I need to see, I ask God to show me what I need to know and he will bring it forth. Usually within a 48-hour period. What a sense of humor my God has. (LoL) Let me also add, this method of communicating with my higher power has never failed me. I remember asking God on a Wednesday to show me what I need to know. A few days prior to finding the picture, something seemed off and I had a feeling something wasn't quite right. Well by Saturday, God answered. My world as I knew it, changed in that instant. The happily ever was no more.

Butch and I met at work ten years prior to our daughter's birth, so we had history. In my mind, our daughter was still an infant and we haven't even taken a family portrait yet. Back in the day when Sears and Roebuck offered the one hundred picture family portrait special, that you so proudly pass out to family and friends as a new mom. I'm still driving, mad and hurt, saying to myself, *you have the time and the nerve to take pictures with another woman sitting on your lap?* My mind was racing but I knew however this went down, I reminded myself that I still have to work on Monday. I drove to my hair appointment, sitting in the chair mad, confused, crying and praying to God. How dare he do this!!!!!! I should have turned my car around because I ended up with blonde hair, not my best look. (yikes)

On the drive back home, I kept asking myself what am I going to do? What should I do? I was trying to play the scene out in my head. I wondered what would happen when I showed him the picture. Talking to myself and God, I asked God for clarity and God showed me by letting me remember, "you've seen this woman before". This was the same woman I had seen a few weeks earlier at the bowling alley and the encounter seemed a little strange, a little tense for someone I didn't know but he clearly did. It felt as if he was trying to keep us away from each other. (more on this later).

As I was driving home from my appointment, an approximately forty-five-minute ride, I decided the relationship was over. I decided to call the police and tell them I have a situation, I'm about to confront someone and we have an infant in the home and I will need him to leave the house immediately. I did not want to hear any lies because this was the same woman I had seen a few weeks prior at the bowling alley when his family came to visit.

His family member and he were behaving strangely and it became clear that this member was familiar and friendly with her, which led me to believe they had met her before. The primary reason for calling the police was that I wasn't sure how he would respond, and I didn't want him to take our daughter out of the house or leave in the car I was financially responsible for. It all happened in a flash. I arrived at the apartment a few minutes before the police and showed Butch the picture and asked him, what is this? He mumbled something, which I knew was no part of the truth and I told him he had to go, *now*. Once the police arrived, I showed them the same picture and I said "see the girl in this picture, on his lap? This is not me". The police allowed him to pack a few things and he left with them. I looked in my baby's eyes, like, now what? Like I stated before, it all happened in a flash. To some it may seem like a small indiscretion, that could have been worked out. There were a few other questionable incidents prior to this day, that did not add up and at this particular moment, the questions I previously dismissed in my head became crystal clear to me. I had a frame of reference on how he moved and when he was not being truthful. After the dust settled and I had a moment to think, and said to myself., "What the hell just happened here"? At that moment, I wasn't thinking about co-parenting or visitations. It never dawned on me to deny a relationship between Taí and her dad, but for us it was a wrap.

We always hear how communication is the key to getting along. What we don't realize is that we're always communicating in some way and our daughters are watching us. Whether we communicate in a loving way or whether we are silent, rolling our eyes, arguing, fussing, or posting our feelings and moods on social media, children see and feel all of this. There will be many times when you may need to take a minute and disconnect from everything in order to regroup. When life throws you curveballs, and you forget to move out the way we must find ways to care for ourselves and in the process, teach our daughters how to take care of themselves as well.

Lesson- Take time to regroup, give yourself time to think and pray before you act or act out.

Chapter 2

❧

Mom First

Being a mom is a gift and a blessing. It is a forever connection that is unmatched by any other relationship. I've held various job titles throughout my working career. Being called *Mom*, by far is the most important title that I'm proud to answer to. When I look back, I can describe it as knowing and loving a soul before you ever see it. It's charting territory unknown, but a mother's love will willingly go before you to guide the way. It's cleaning the scrapes and bruises, it guidance and protection. A mom can look beyond your faults and see your needs. It's a love that encourages the best and when your best falls short, mom says it's okay. You are enough just as you are.

Being a mom is a journey, it can take you in many directions, as well as challenge you to look at life through a new lens. Motherhood also helped me find a new purpose. I always asked myself, what's at stake if we mess this parenting thing up? Her *heart* was always my comeback answer. What will she say and how will she feel years from now? The *"end adult"* matters most, is what I tell myself.

Being a mom at the age of thirty- one made me feel like I needed to bring my "A" game. Our children look up to us. As a mom you may or may not care about his absence or his presence, depending on the nature of the relationship between the two of you, but your daughter certainly will. We are socially conditioned and wired as humans with a need to know both biological parents. This could further explain why some children who are adopted may vigilantly look for their birth parents, no matter how great their adoptive parents are. Our parents are our first indoctrination into our traditions, culture, habits, and spirituality. They give us our first world view.

Patterns of the way the family is formed has changed over several decades. It may or may not be the norm in *your* community to be raised by both parents. If it is the norm to have both parents in the household, you can rest assured that your daughter is aware that her family may look differently from her friends' if dad is not there.

The flipside of these experiences is your daughter can develop a determined spirit, resilience, empathy, and incredible survival skills despite the relationship or lack thereof with her dad. In addition, she can go on to grow, thrive, succeed, love and be loved. Not left to chance, I often sought out and encouraged activities that I thought would help her develop her sense of self, and teach her how to cope with life and its challenges. Our resilience is shaped in part from our personalities, genes, temperament and the environment we grow up in.

Parents can begin in the home, by providing opportunities that build their child's confidence and help them learn how to deal with obstacles, successes and failures. This in turn, can build resilience. You can help your child by incorporating the following tools:

- help build up their confidence by taking on personal challenges (educational or sports related goals).

- help them learn how to identify, express and manage their emotions, which can also be essential to learning how to self-regulate (when they can make these distinctions, it helps them worry less and focus more).

- help build positive relationships with other peers and adults (having the capacity to form and maintain relationships is essential to them and how to function within society. Also a key component to being mentally healthy). These are stepping stones to assist them in meeting life's challenges into adolescence and adulthood.

Lesson- Moms, look for ways that help build, prepare and strengthen.

Chapter 3

⌒

My Road Dog

Breakups just generally suck, your emotions are all over the place. You may fall into a funk, cry a lot, live in your pajamas, just overall feel out of sorts, although the breakup may have been the best thing at the time. When you breakup in your 20's without having a child, you may have the luxury of only going to work and back to bed. When you have to function as a mom, her needs came first and that much needed breakdown has to wait. Not having friends and family nearby, my daughter became my road dog. I had a weekday sitter, but I did not want to impose on her on the weekends. We resumed our routine. I took Taí shopping, hair salons, doctor visits, nails, you name it. I found businesses that were child friendly. You remind yourself it's going to be okay and keep it moving.

She was almost 7 months old, babies adapt pretty well. She wasn't able to ask, hey where's that fun guy who used to hold me, play with me and feed me? I felt like she was looking at me, I told myself I must bring my A game (whatever that was).

Butch moved back near his hometown about two hours away, he called and tried to visit Taí whenever he could. I always encouraged contact of any kind.

Lesson- Exhale often, be kind to yourself,
and love and honor yourself.

Chapter 4

~

UNME (Understanding the Now Means Everything)

When I think of raising daughters in today's society;I think of the challenges, the responsibilities and the many pressures there are just for them to "be". These challenges were different twenty years ago. The skills it takes to balance and grow into one's positive self as a young woman in today's society of "show me your pretty" have been magnified by the introduction and acceptability of social media.

Our girls need to feel secure in themselves. Our girls need to be able to make good decisions, make positive choices about their lives and learn how to express their thoughts and feelings. Our girls should also learn to care about others and realize all lives matter. There were times growing up when I saw her insecurities and self-doubt kick in. It's during these times I would talk to her, offer her encouragement and find activities she could engage herself in and develop a "can do" attitude.

Thankfully our community offered a host of activities. I tried to find activities that would boost her self-esteem and resilience. She was able to join and find activities where she learned about music, sports, sign language, or attend girl empowerment workshops. There were times when I saw her confidence take a dive and I would talk to her and offered her encouragement.

As young women grow and develop, we have all experienced at one time or another feeling like a member of the *"Un" club,* especially during adolescence when you are trying to find your independence and identity. By being a member of the *UNME* club, I describe it as feelings of being:

Unwanted

Unworthy

Unlovable

Unimportant

Unattractive

Unacceptable

What we don't want, is our daughters to stay paralyzed in that place because she hasn't yet realized it will be okay, as we provide the tools she needs to navigate out of her comfort zone, to find out just how awesome she can be. As parents we try to protect our children from having bad or painful memories, but we can only try to minimize them and create occasions that will foster better memories. I have many mottos that I ascribe to. However, when

I talk about parenting, especially with her dad and others dads, I always say "create memories"; spend quality time with her and try to foster those things and activities that will build courage, strength, positive self-esteem, resilience and build good character.

Lesson-Teach her, encourage her to believe in her value and her worth.

Chapter 5

~

Different Dreams

In your alone time after a break up, there are a million scenes on replay. A friend of mine, says when it comes to breakups, she prefers to "cut it and let it bleed" (no friendship, no communication). Everyone will respond differently, especially when a child is involved. You will also realize in this process, you must get different dreams about your future. Healing is a process, and requires some space, both physical and mental. Allow yourself time to heal and if it's important to you, try to build or maintain a healthy relationship with the only other person who loves your daughter as much as you (her dad). You must know the relationship going forward will ebb and flow, and this too is okay.

I concluded that my experience happened for a reason, and one of my lessons was to learn to trust my intuition. It is my belief that everyone who shows up in our life, shows up to teach us something about them or to teach us something about ourselves, in our case we both learned a lot. I try to view situations that don't work out, not as failures, just lessons learned (God's protection).

If anything, ask yourself what is the lesson you needed to learn from that encounter with that certain someone. The lessons could be about love, tolerance, truth, resilience etc. This is where I learned to compartmentalize my life, after all, I still had a little one to care for. I had to steal time to take care of my emotional and physical well-being.

Being keenly aware that how you feel about the other parent, may also affect your parenting. This is where you begin to repair, rebuild, and reset. I had to think about our new rules of engagement. After all, Taí didn't need to be privy to our "shenanigans". Over the years Butch and I have had a few highly charged "disrespectful"moments. However in the same day I could later share a funny story with Taí about her dad. Again compartmentalizing when I needed to. There was the man I once wanted to build a life with and the man I occasionally disliked intensely.

I made a point of keeping the door open for him to join this co-parenting pool, where the water wasn't always warm and clean, but I kept reminding myself, we are "family".

Lesson- Welcome new beginnings. They provide opportunities to grow.

Chapter 6

∼

The Elephant in The Room

As life would have it, sometimes things just don't work out. Depending on the age of your daughter, and when you parted as a couple, not talking about her dad can bring up a sense of loss or even grief if ignored. It may even create a sense of shame. Your daughter may think to herself, he must be bad, or dad doesn't matter because we don't even talk about him. While parenting, you must acknowledge your own feelings about how you parent without the other parent around, while helping her manage her own feelings. How you feel and relate to her dad, is very important.

Try not to speak negatively about him to your daughter, be conscious of the tone of your voice and the expressions on your face. (That wicked side eye) I always heard time waits for no one, and I've found that to be so true. Remember where you are currently will not be where you end up and situations will undoubtedly change over time, good, bad or indifferent. You cannot control the change, but you can control how you respond.

My friends and I were at different stages of single parenting, some due to divorce, some death of a spouse or dealing with dads who were in and out, emotionally and physically. Bored one night while our daughters were still infants, my friend Sam and I called the Psychic Hotline. Those were the days of Miss Cleo, whose famous tagline was "call me nowww". My ladies in their forties and fifties may remember the commercial with Miss Cleo. We called to talk about our failed relationships, just for fun of course. My psychic must have had the "gift " fortunately or unfortunate for me because she was a little more accurate than my friend Sam's. She shared with me that she saw another child somewhere which later turned out to be true. Unbeknownst to me at the time, she was referring to the child Butch fathered after our relationship ended. Sam's psychic was a little more humorous and had little to no information for her. She said to Sam something like hey what's up? What's up with you? The psychic said hey girl, I'm fine. Sam said "Helloooooooooo that's why I'm calling you! We still laugh at that today. Just having a silly mom moment.

Looking back, Sam probably had the best arrangement logistically, not so much emotionally. Sam had financial support and shared a predictable weekly co-parenting schedule. However the emotional connection of raising a newborn with a man who couldn't or didn't love Sam in the way she needed was a constant dagger in the heart. As she describes it, it was almost like a business arrangement. He would pick up his daughter weekly as scheduled, exchanging hellos and necessary information about the baby and be gone until drop off time again. Unfortunately, there was never enough comforting or clever girlfriend words to make her situation easier. Looking back at the most important quality, the fact that he was a present and responsible father was a good deal. She practiced patience, acceptance, and compartmentalizing her situation, accepting that it is, what it is.

Sam said she prayed to God throughout her pregnancy to let her daughter's father always be there for them, whether they were together or not. She technically got what she prayed for. Although their relationship did not work out at the time, he was and is still sharing parental responsibilities today. We may need to be a little more specific when talking to God about who we have children with. (Lol) We made play dates, shared tips on how to save time on housework and shared other helpful new mom tips. Hire a service or someone to clean for you, have a girlfriend cleaning day, where you can exchange duties and barter for future services. Have a kid's sleepover so the other moms can have some needed alone "mommy time". Using my village served to bring some peace at the end of some crazy days.

My daughter was around ten years old when I started a parenting group through Parent's Anonymous in my area. This is a non-profit organization in our area where parents are provided with support, a sense of community, belonging and trust. They also offer training for the youth and parents that can help them transform their behaviors, attitudes and build on strengths to make positive changes. We met once a week to discuss the different nuances of parenting and support each other. Both men and women attended at the time.

My friend Cecilia is the mother of two young boys when she got divorced. Their marital relationship was very tumultuous for many years. When they parted, he was in and out of his boys' lives, mostly out. He would make promises he didn't keep. He struggled with substance abuse issues. She always talked about a special prayer she would say every night before she put her children to bed. Her prayer was, to let God let her live until her sons reach the legal age of adulthood, which is eighteen. The purpose behind this prayer was, if something unfortunate happened to her, they could care for themselves and choose how to involve their father in their life. The drama with their dad at times was too much to bear and the thought of him raising them gave her anxiety.

I didn't really understand that concept of what she was praying for until I needed to, and her words rang out so loud and so clear to me one day. Parenting is a lifetime journey. Situations can go from good to bad in what seems like an instant. I found myself repeating her same prayer often, during our bad times of trying to co-parent, during times when he would disappear or be active in his addiction. I would silently pray, God please let me live at least until my daughter turns 18 years old, so she will be able to live on her own care for herself and choose how she wanted her father to be a part of her life.

Lesson- A mother's love wants the best for her children, recognizing that in love, you may need to protect them from the other parent.

Chapter 7

~

Dad's Addiction

Let me start by sharing, writing this chapter was hard. What makes it a little easier, is that Butch owns his story. He is comfortable sharing his story and has given me permission to do the same. Even the most loving and caring parent once they are entangled in the cycle of addiction and recovery can be hard to accept and deal with. In between the lies, inconsistency, the deceit, the unavailability, the manipulation, broken promises and lack of respect, he is still family to your daughter. How do we treat family? We try to help them, we try to encourage them, at times we keep them close and sometimes we need distance between us and them. Many times dealing with an addict, you struggle with how to help and sometimes nothing helps. This struggle has been off and on for over 20 years.

Butch is a college graduate, hall of fame recipient in his hometown for track and field and hard worker. He has a personality that people are drawn to, a fun-loving side of him and most who meet him would say he's a good friend and all around good guy.

We made a choice to not share his addiction with our daughter. I knew the day would come but I wasn't sure when. Not until she went off to college did I encourage him to tell her. I chose this time in her life because she was beginning to question herself. She would say, "what was it about me that he keeps breaking promises"? or "why can't he show up for me"? He often broke his promises and would go without contact for weeks at a time.

Butch's addiction was easier to hide because he wasn't living in the area, he has moved several times since she was little. There were many times that he was in and out and she had questions and I had many excuses on deck for his absence. What I began to notice was that Taí was beginning to talk openly and internalize his behavior and how it made her feel. Not knowing exactly what the "it" was, she would tell herself that's just "how he is". Sometimes it was hard for me to recognize when he was using. Through it all, he was always welcome in our home. He was always invited to attend important events when he could. When she was younger and he made promises he couldn't keep, I would buy gifts and cards and sign his name to them. I would encourage him to keep in touch. It causes you to be the bigger person, you're not fighting against the person, your fighting with what the addiction has caused them to become.

When it comes to discussing any parent's addiction I would offer this. Keep it age appropriate, the level of detail you choose to provide will depend on the age of your child and their level of maturity. Keep it as honest as you can because children can often tell when adults are lying to them. You can explain how addiction is a disease caused by many factors. You may share that there is treatment available but ultimately mom or dad needs to be ready to accept the help. Something I'm pretty sure I didn't do well, was to acknowledge the impact his addiction had and still has on her. Off and on by Butch sharing his life story of how he grew up and openly acknowledge his feelings to her, it put things in perspective for her. Lastly, he has let her know he will answer any question she has but I'm not to sure if she's taking full advantage. She takes in what she can handle and processes it accordingly. If you look at research and the genetics of drug and alcohol addiction, it will state that addiction is 50 percent due to genetic predisposition and 50 percent due to poor coping skills, such as dealing with stress or uncomfortable emotions, this according to addictions and recovery.org.[1] The good news is that our genes are not our destiny. Lots of people come from addicted families and live happy and fulfilled lives. A few important facts to know is that addiction has a cycle and it is a disease. It is something a person will need to manage daily for as long as they are living. There is no easy fix and addicts take it one day at a time. Recovery is an option, not a cure. As previously stated, her dad is not just his addiction. Forgiveness is always an option and not being an enabler to those you love and care about takes practice. You want your daughter to learn healthy coping skills for herself.

As Taí becomes older, this will undoubtedly challenge her trust with him. If a parent's addiction is not acknowledged, it can begin another generational cycle of addiction, causing the same ill

1 addictionsandrecovery.org

effects in the daughter's relationship, children of addicts may experience loneliness, guilt, anxiety, poor self-image, and depression. Daughters with fathers who are in and out of their lives or absent altogether, may struggle to maintain and build their own relationships. According to an article written by Robert Thurston (June 2015). Girls may develop an eating disorder, and may become sexually active earlier and may be susceptible to addiction issues themselves.

Lessons- Addiction is a family disease. One person may use, but the whole family suffers.

Chapter 8

∽

In the Meantime/Growing Pains

While Taí was in middle School going into high school, Butch moved back into this area to be closer to her which didn't turn out well for him. Unbeknownst to him while attempting to change his surroundings (people, places, and things), he moved into an area which set his addiction back by leaps and bounds.

High School was her most difficult time as she tried navigating the nuances of new friends, changing of old friends, dating, new teachers and new exposures. During this time, she and her dad were still trying to find common ground and peace within their relationship. During this time, Taí experienced her share of hurt, anger and confusion.

She struggled with his presence, as well as his absence. Our community is small, so she witnessed some erratic behaviors as well as heard some things through friends in school. She shrugged it off, and told herself " that's just him". His struggle is real. During this time, he was in and out of county jail for traffic issues which turned into holdovers for child support issues. Like most addicts, his life had become unmanageable right before my eyes.

During this time, I dealt with situations as they came, on a need to know basis. Moms, there is no right or wrong way to handle these situations. Keep the lines of communication between you and her. You know your daughters' temperament and personality, and what she can handle. Adjust as you need to.

Seek out organizations such as Narcotics Anonymous and Nar-Anon, which are self help organizations to assist families who have loved ones coping with substance abuse problems. (I did not) At different stages in her development she needed different responses from me. For example, during her childhood, she would show signs of wanting to be independent, being self-conscious about her body and hiding her emotions with her "game face". During these times, I would offer her encouragement and reassurance that I was here if she needed me and she could always count on me. Acknowledge your daughter's struggles with empathy by putting them in perspective, while assuring her feelings of awkwardness would pass.

Tai's adolescence turned out to be a little more challenging as most young people who try to figure it out and test parental boundaries. She showed inclinations of moodiness, being conscious of her body and all while trying to figure out where she fit in. During this time, I tried to hear her concerns, listen to her opinions, while setting limits and impose fair rules and be supportive. I'm sure to her I was the meanest parent. I recently learned she would reach out to her father when she wanted to go someplace and I said she couldn't. She would call and say to him, "She said no again, she always says no, I can't do anything". He would listen and try to tell her being out every weekend was not necessary or offer some other words of comfort, without trying to challenge my authority. I was that Friday night to and from pick-up mom from the movies, from the party, from whatever activity she attended. Still not sure why our versions of her full social calendar are different.

In hindsight there were several things I would have done differently. My advice is to deal with those bumps as they come, don't be discouraged. Knowing your daughter's temperament may also determine how you interact with and correct her.

> *Lesson-Teach her how to tolerate discomfort, it teaches self-regulation and strengthens her confidence.*

Chapter 9

~

College Days

The day Taí was going to college he was being released from the county jail and called as we were planning to drive her to her dorm. It was at this point Butch and I had a candid conversation about his drug use and the residual that we deal with. I explained to him, she is questioning herself, wondering if it was it something about her, is the reason why he kept not showing up for her? I said something like, "he has a story to tell you, which might explain some things". I can't quite remember what I said to her, but I placed a call to him and he said he will handle it.

A few months into her college days, Butch went to visit her at college and had "the talk" with her about his addiction. She repeated some of what he said, but I'm not sure if she really understood it at that time. She said it was nice to know and answered a few questions for her. I believe she was able to understand that it had little to do with her and more about him. He had a way of inserting humor with even the most serious topics, he was always viewed as fun dad and easily forgiven. During her formative years, many areas were affected by her dad's addiction. While dealing with an addiction, the children move to the back burner. Ironically and currently my daughter is working in a recovery program for women and children after completing graduate school. To say it's been an eye opener is an understatement. She's learning how powerful addictions can be, and how children become a casualty of that war as well as the off and on struggle of recovery.

Lesson- Trust your instincts, you will know when the time is right.

Chapter 10

~

Maternal Gatekeeping

I came across this term while conducting research for my workshop called Letters To My Daughter. The subject matter referenced, when dad lives elsewhere. This term refers to a mother's protective beliefs about the desirability of a father's involvement in the child's life and the behaviors acted upon that either facilitate or hinder collaborative child rearing or co-parenting between the parents. You may be able to relate to this based on the skills you believe your child's father has or does not have.

Simply put, mom wonders if dad can take care of their daughter as well as she does when she's not around. For obvious reasons, I wasn't sure of his ability to co-parent even during his "clean time". Dad's house, dad's rules and dad's life will be different from yours and you may shed some tears and have to pray often on this co-parenting journey. The lines of communication should be open for the child to express their thoughts and feelings. The goal is to lessen the chance of miscommunication, resentments and avoid conflicts as everyone continues to adjust.

This was the case with my friend LaLa after her divorce. As per the court order, the children had to go to their dad's house every other weekend. She was unsure of his parenting skills and he was not open to any advice from LaLa, while the children were in his care. If something occurred, she could not comfortably intervene or call to discuss anything with him, because it would quickly escalate into a shouting match, on the smallest of issues. She later said fear kept her from filing for sole custody and looking back she questioned would that have benefited the children? Nevertheless, the family endured for six years and made it to the other side of young adulthood, where the children are now older and thriving in college. The other side is, the children learned to deal with their dad in their own way, on their terms and resolve the conflicts as needed. Their dad learned from them as well. *We teach people how to treat us.*

Lesson-Don't focus on things you can't control, it paralyzes your power as a parent.

Chapter 11

~

Court/ Your Honor
May I Speak?

These issues can go as smooth as silk or can drive you to drink or somewhere in the middle. Fortunately, my court days were few, maybe three appearances if I remember correctly. I encourage everyone to mediate, negotiate or re- evaluate with each other first, if you can without the court's involvement. You can find yourself in a tailspin between courts dates, attorney fees, delays and unsettled mediations.

Experiencing a divorce can be messy. These proceedings can bring out the best and worst in individuals. My friend LaLa, said it took a few years to stop hearing the boots of her ex walk through the house, after their divorce. The sound of boots in her head would cause her to sit up straight in the bed, and cause her anxiety attacks. It's been six years since their divorce and she stills feels a little bitter and guilty for what the children had to go through. Just know its normal to blame yourself and feel a little guilty. While your children are young there may be many battles over the years involving attending sporting activities together, who will attend parent teacher conferences, friends, grades, extra-curricular activities, switching days of visitation, chores etc. Naturally, your protective motherly instinct will be in overdrive.

During these times we would pray together, talk until the wee hours, talk each other off the ledge and remind each other that "doing prison time" for bodily harm would not solve the problem. (LoL) When you calm down, try to examine the situation from all sides, every situation may not be cause for extreme reactions. You must pace yourself, this is a journey. I would try to assure her, he wouldn't harm them, he's doing the best he knows how and they have each other. LaLa, spent countless dollars on attorney fees during her divorce; while also taking time off from work to have lawyers negotiate because talking to each other and agreeing on certain matters did not work for them, only to have him later disregard as he saw fit. There were job related factors as well as finances that kept her from seeking enforcement of the divorce decree every time he disregarded the agreement. There were several instances where both parents attended an event and her ex frequently made a scene. She choose to be the bigger person and physically distance herself as to not cause a bigger scene for her children. It was during these times, she looked within and relied on inner strength, using her sister friends and realized she had to pick her battles.

Lesson- How you feel about the other parent is less important than how you act toward him.

Chapter 12

~

Custody /I Need a Ride to the Courthouse

Butch and I never needed a formal custody agreement and then one day out of the blue, I received papers regarding custody. Of course panic was my first emotion. First of all, I NEVER knew I had to obtain custody for someone I gave birth to, however New Jersey said differently. A few days before court, he called to tell me he didn't have a ride, and would I mind giving him a ride. I replied, surely you jest. WHAT IN THE? Was he serious? I said to myself, you want me to pick up up, so you can sue me for custody? I couldn't sleep the night before because I was unsure of what to expect. I had heard all the horror stories about the unfairness about family court horror, and know a few friends who are still healing from their "court wounds" years later. I showed up to court Butch did not, and I obtained "sole legal custody" of Tai'. As for the finances, we had an order for child support which had been in place since she was an infant, however the money was inconsistent, depending on his employment status at the time. Thankfully I had full time employment. The money became more consistent while Taí was in college and until after she graduated. It helped maintain her while in school, which took a load off my household. Off and on, he would fill in with other items that certainly helped also.

Sometimes the money is not the only factor to consider while co-parenting. When I decided to enter into "forever" with (Sallie Mae) for student loans and return back to school to obtain my master's in clinical counseling in Psychology, I needed my "village" (Darn those radio commercials luring people to go back to school). My family was very supportive. I often took Taí to class with me, she made friends with the cafeteria lady and ate many free pretzels, while I attended class. She later remembered and wrote about our experience. Taí ate many dinners in the car, while I rushed to class or was watched and fed by neighbors. One night Butch offered to watch her while I attended class. He was attempting to fix her spaghetti for dinner. However, he hit the bottom of the jar, and the sauce accidentally spilled all over my kitchen. I wondered why for weeks I often saw red spots in various parts of my kitchen, neither one of them said a thing. A funny memory they still share today.

Lesson-Spending time and creating memories is one of the greatest gifts a father can give a child.

Chapter 13

~

Setting Boundaries

My husband, Bey was *very* tolerant when it came to boundaries with Butch. We married when she was four years old. He was always supportive of me and the way I chose to handle our co-parenting situation between all of us, even when he disagreed. He always sought to find a way to turn a negative situation into a positive. His children from a previous marriage live out of state, so he was unable to co-parent with his ex. Demonstrating a healthy co-parenting relationship helps your child recognize how important they are to the both of you.

I know setting boundaries is easier said than done. I know first hand what it's like if you've ever seen your child stand at the door or window and wait for the visit that never happens, or wondering why dad missed an event or waiting for the phone to ring, its nothing short of heartbreaking. Just to prevent seeing the pain in your daughter's eyes, you may be tempted to cut all ties. However, if the next time you talk to him and he can reassure you he will be there. Like myself, you may be inclined to give him another chance. There is no playbook for parenting. It is truly on the job training. My goal was always try to keep the connection.

Tai' later said at her own graduation, watching me go through the struggle of working, going to school, and having a family gave her motivation to continue her education and continue to always grow. She said, and I quote; *"you made sure I got to witness that moment. From sitting with you in classes and making sure that I was fed and still made sure I had hobbies of my own; you did it with such grace, thank you for always encouraging me to work smarter and to continue my education"*. Side note, (KIDS NOTICE EVERY-THING) she obtained her Bachelor's degree from Rutgers University and her Master of Social Work from Howard University.

Children don't necessarily remember money or material things, they do remember the time spent with their parents and other adults who make them feel valued. I always told Butch and every man I speak to who have children **"Create the memories"**. Butch thanked my husband at Tai's college graduation party in front of friends and family. He said "thank you for being there when I couldn't". Taí said it made her feel proud that over the years, we always made the effort to get along.

Lesson- There is the right thing to do and the "heart thing" to do. Choose carefully.

Chapter 14

~

Hair Drama

Another woman knows, and a father may quickly learn how a mom feels about another woman doing their daughter's hair. This can be a fight like no other. A way to navigate this would be to put her hair in a style that will last throughout the visit such as braids or a ponytail. You may have to show him how to do her hair. I tried on a few occasions but he couldn't quite get the hang of it.

Butch would take Taí to his sister's house, she had four girls, so they would just fall in line for the hair torture session. She would always come back with those tight ponytails with the plastic balls on them, so tight sometimes she would need a Tylenol. We still laugh about that today.

Taking her to the bathroom was tricky, he said he would stand outside the door. She said "mom we were usually with his girlfriend at the time and she would escort me in". Because you are the primary caretaker, you feel like you know what's best, sometimes unintentionally not allowing room for him to come in and learn.

Lesson-Teach him and show him.

Chapter 15

~

I Don't Eat That

Food is another important area in which communication is key. When dad is not in the house, it's incumbent upon you to communicate with him about the child's dietary needs, allergies, little quirks etc. It could save the day.

My daughter did not eat white bread when she was younger. Butch had taken her to the beach and packed sandwiches on white bread. In our house we only ate potato bread, he says I don't remember you telling me that. Our generation grew up on Wonder Bread (those over the age of forty know this all-purpose bread, good for sandwiches, used in place of hotdog and hamburger rolls, an all-purpose bread). He pulls out his prepared sandwiches for the day on the beach; she said "Dad, I don't eat white bread". In his words, he became more than a little annoyed. It was 100 degrees outside, he's walking up and down the boardwalk in search of potato bread. Not sure why it never dawned on him to go to a Seven Eleven or another convenience store. That was a simple example, nevertheless important when it came to feeding her. The same with McDonald's Happy Meals, she didn't like Happy Meals. They still laugh about that memory today.

Lesson-Communication sometimes can make the little things stay little things.

Chapter 16

~

Apology Accepted

The power of a sincere apology is often underestimated. Parents make mistakes and often do not live up to the "super hero" image our children may have of us. In turn, parents often experience feelings of guilt and or shame when we don't live up to the expectations we have for ourselves. If a parent misses a scheduled visit or makes a promise they can't keep, encourage them to apologize to the child. Not only does it hold that parent accountable, but allows her to voice her disappointment directly. Hopefully disappointment is not a feeling, the child will become used to. In any case, recognizing and validating the child's feelings, as well as changing the behaviors can help. It can also offer restoration to a fractured, relationship, along with learning how to forgive.

If the child is apprehensive in communicating their feelings, as kids often are, mom can explain to dad how it hurts the child's feelings.

Depending on the age of the child, he or she may become more empathetic of their parent's imperfections. If a parent's behavior is toxic, and/or puts the child at risk or harm by all means error on the side of safety and protect your child. You must be the force field around your child. As the primary parent, you decide when the force field goes up and when it comes down.

Lesson- Changed behavior is the best apology.

Chapter 17

~

How She Feels Matters

This is not to criticize single moms or to blame non custodial fathers, but sometimes we just miss the mark, if there is no collaboration, there is no co-parenting. Accommodations must be made. The point is, both parents' involvement is critical to children's overall well-being. In our case, I have to give credit to Butch, no matter what he was going through, he will end each conversation with Taí with "I love you", and she feels it. Dad's presence should give your daughter a good feeling and a view of what a positive expression of love feels like. It should encourage her to love and appreciate herself.

Whenever possible, I tried to keep him in the loop about what was going on in her life. My daughter said her friends always thought it was cool how he could come over and hang out with her. She appreciated that he could come over and spend time while her friends were there, or spend a few minutes with my husband watching a game. Be flexible.

This became our normal. Hopefully, if my daughter is ever faced with a similar situation in her future, she will have a blueprint to navigate with.

> *Lesson-Jump right on in, the parenting pool is always open. You can never go wrong by doing what's right.*

Chapter 18

∾

Bigger Than my Bitterness

One of the many lessons I've learned about parenting, is that parenting takes maturity as well as the ability to be flexible. Standing strong in a wrong, does not serve anyone. Parents should be open to shifting their thinking.

Take the high road, no negative talking about the other parent to the child. From your child's' point of view, if you are speaking bad about the other parent, you are speaking bad about someone who is a part of them. While in each other's presence, try to put a lid on any feelings of anguish, anger, or betrayal you may be harboring. Children pickup on moods and attitudes. Children need your consistency, it makes them feel safe.

It's not required that as separated parents you also be friends but it can help, along with mutual respect. At a minimum, keep the lines of communication open regarding matters of importance such as school progress, sickness, hospital visits, events, changes in your daughter's mood or attitude.

My husband has children from his first marriage. One of them was injured in a car accident, he was not made aware of this accident until he received paperwork from the insurance company, as he was the parent providing insurance for them. Of course he was hurt by not be informed, but there wasn't much he could do because their mom made a choice not to tell him and they lived out of the state at the time. He always provided financial and medical care. He would also visit them several times a year from a very young age until they graduated high school. He stated that our union and coparenting situation brought to light just how much he missed out on with his biological children, and how much more could have been done if he and their mother were able to communicate differently and put aside their differences for the sake of the children.

I realized that early on whatever Butch could offer was bigger than my bitterness. The patches were *very* rough and disheartening at times, but we made it through the other side.

Lesson- Work on fixing the problem, not the blame.

Chapter 19

❧

My Village/ My Saviors

I had to learn, there is nothing selfish about self care and you must be intentional about taking care of you. Moms, you must learn to take care of you, *always in all ways*. I like to read, talk with my sister friends, do a little retail therapy and just sit in a quiet space. A friend once told me, she had to design her balanced life. I asked her how do I begin, she simply said "start by making purposeful choices that feed your mind, your body and your soul". This lesson was consciously passed on to my daughter. She watched me take mental health days off from work, meditate, attend workshops that empower women, listen to music to change my energy, and do whatever I had to do to restore and recharge. Replenish your temple with good thoughts, good food and good care. Be careful who you let in your circle. Of course, this comes with the experience of living, but some relationships, male and female, can drain your energy. You are the captain of your ship and sometimes the ship needs to be refueled. Are you putting in regular gas, mid-grade or premium? Each part of your temple needs attention and re-fueling. Check in with yourself, investigate these areas of your life and see what needs tweaking.

For example:

- ✓ Choices you make and friendships- look at who is in your circle. Do they drain you, support you, or use you?

- ✓ Staying "strong in your wrong"- ask yourself, can I think of a different outcome/situation, instead of saying this is how I've always done it?

- ✓ Socialization- ask yourself, how do I entertain myself? How often do I meet with friends? What recharges your low energy? Check your spiritual tank.

- ✓ Improving communication skills-do I need to rethink the way I ask for what I need or want? Am I intentional or do I go with the flow? Am I mean spirited when things don't go my way?

- ✓ Getting emotionally healthy- ask yourself are there some life areas that you may need to talk to a mental health professional about. Depression, PTSD, eating disorders, old childhood wounds/scars, anger or anxiety?

- ✓ Value check- are you living your truth, are you thinking one way, but your behaviors reflect differently?

- ✓ Annual check-ups- when was the last time you had a good medical check up? Are you aware of those health issues that run in your family history? (mental as well as physical disorders).

Luckily, I've always had a few good girlfriends to lean on. Good friends let you cry on their shoulder and talk endlessly about the same or similar parenting struggles and provide support. Even if you haven't met that "good Judy" or have an OLG (old lady gang) with whom you can drink and spill the tea, it's still important to put *on your oxygen mask* from time to time. Think about it, if you don't take care of yourself properly, you won't be able to care for those who need you most.

Lesson- Don't be afraid to ask for help when you need it. Put your own oxygen mask on first. You can't help others until you help yourself first.

Chapter 20

~

God Got Me

I found a church that was child friendly where I could participate in service and keep my daughter with me without worrying about her in the "infant room" or child care center. For those who are unfamiliar with this, some churches have different rooms to care for the children, separating the children from the parents, in order for them to enjoy the service without distractions. My church had a big, soundproof glass in the back of the church where you could see the service and the kids were in the same room with you, but couldn't be heard. What a life saver!! I found peace and solace by attending church. Since my college days, wherever I moved, I always found a church home. I've been attending church all of my life.

This church was different for me, in that it acknowledged and addressed the areas of need for the members. Most Sundays Bishop Donald Hilliard Jr., current Bishop of Cathedral International in Perth Amboy, N.J., would take up an offering and designate it to the single mothers, the unemployed or senior citizens in the church. I always felt a sense of peace and inclusion when I left the service, my daughter and I eventually joined and got baptized at the church.

Lesson-Having peace within is a gift you can always give to yourself.

Chapter 21

∼

Breathe in and Exhale Often.

My spirituality has always been important to me. There are many ways to express your spirituality. I choose prayer, meditation and affirmations. I have many prayers that I've come to rely on. The Serenity Prayer was always one of my favorites. It says; "God grant me the serenity to accept the things I cannot change, the courage to change the things I can and the wisdom to know the difference". This prayer is utilized in the Alcoholics Anonymous community and other twelve step programs. I heard this prayer over thirty years ago and somehow it spoke to all I needed and wanted to say.

Journaling your thoughts is also another way to exhale, explore feelings, prioritize your goals and take a private look at areas in your life. It helps to calm and clear your mind. I also find that journaling changes my energy in a positive way. Within my writings, I find clarity and healing.

Lesson-Choose a positive method to express yourself and show your daughter the same.

Chapter 22

∾

Cry Showers/Water Can Be Healing

Crying in the shower provided an emotional release from the days where I found myself frustrated, angry or needed to ease the emotional pain of life events. When my friend LaLa became a new mom, I shared this little tip with her because like most new moms, she was feeling a lot of uncertainty, stress, anxiety or all of the above. You may not want to sniffle and sob in front of your daughter. It's been over twenty years, and we still chuckle about the "cry showers".

One of my personal mottos is "there's more room out than in". Keeping your emotions bottled in is not good for one's health. A good cry tends to make you feel better.

Lesson- Water has healing powers.

Chapter 23

~

Matters that Interfere With My Parenting/Oh Lord Help Me Out Of This Funk

Accordi to Web MD, depression is defined as a *persistent* feeling of sadness and loss of interest in otherwise enjoyable or daily activities, or an emptiness you can't seem to shake. Major or clinical depression is marked by a depressed mood most of the day. These and other symptoms are generally present every day for at least 2 weeks. If you find yourself experiencing extreme fatigue, feelings of worthlessness, insomnia, or hypersomnia (excessive sleeping) or thoughts of death or suicide, seek help immediately at your local hospital or clinic.

Women are twice as likely as men to suffer from depression. Some of the contributing factors are; hormonal changes, menopause and miscarriage. Increased stress at work, home, caring for an aging parent as well as raising a child alone can increase the risk of woman who may already be biologically vulnerable. Mental health has always been a touchy subject to approach and to find common ground in which to talk about safely. Within many communities, especially the African- American community we are just beginning to acknowledge, discuss and seek treatment for mental illness. We must learn to deal with the patterns and pathologies that exist within our community as well as other communities.

Some may view the diagnosis of being depressed as a sign of weakness. Just as our bodies need a break, so does our mind. Most men and women can admit to experiencing feelings of sadness at some point in their lives. Although I never fell into the clinical definition of depression, there were days I did pull the covers over my body and didn't want to come out. My daughter said "Mom, you slept a lot". Some days I wasn't sure what I felt. I would pray to God, just let me get out this funk. I just wanted to do the bare minimum, feed her and jump back into the bed. The covers felt warm and safe.

According to J. Diamond, author of <u>Surviving Male Menopause.</u> <u>A Guide for Women and Men,</u> women and men also respond to *stress* differently. Men often seek an escape activity to get relief from stress and create a relaxation diversion. Men tend to blame others, women tend to blame themselves. Men tend create conflict, women tend avoid conflict. Men may need to feel in control, women may have trouble setting boundaries. Men may use sex, television, or drugs. Women may use food, friends and "love" to self medicate.

The point is, depression and stress can keep us in bad head space as well contribute to unhealthy patterns of behaviors. Seek treatment as needed. Take care of you. You only get one you.

Lesson- Allow yourself to feel and take care of yourself accordingly.

Chapter 24

~

We Can't Choose Our Family, Only Our Friends/ Dad Has Another Child

Not sure which one of us told Taí that she had a brother, but she was made aware in middle school. My daughter is an only child, I thought she should know that she had other family in this world. I wrote Sheila a letter one day and asked if she thought having our children meet would be a good idea. Luckily, she was okay with the idea. Butch did not have a good relationship with Sheila. Sheila and I agreed to meet so I told her next time she's in Jersey to let me know and we'll meet up. She lived out of state.

We had our first awkward meeting at a mall in Northern New Jersey a few months after my letter. It was awkward for us as adults because I had not seen Sheila since the week before my relationship with Butch ended (yep you guessed it, same girl from the picture I found).

When we arrived, Taí and her nine year old brother, Shawn, looked at each other and waved hello, found their way to the nearby seats. Sheila and I sat down and we talked about how nervous both of them were to meet each other. We talked about the kids' interests like sports and school. Taí and Shawn are two years apart in age. She asked me about Butch and said they only speak via phone when family court calls regarding child support. The meetup took about twenty minutes, she said they would be in town a few more days and would head back home. We exchanged telephone numbers and emails and said our polite goodbyes and left the mall. I asked Taí how she felt, she said it was okay, she really didn't talk too much on the way home. I think she needed time to take it all in.

When Taí graduated from high school, I thought it would be a nice surprise to have them meet up again. By this time, there had been some communication back and forth on social media between them. I believe it was Myspace at the time. I reached out to Sheila via email, to see what she thought of the idea. Sheila said she would check with her son and let us know because at that time he had no relationship with his father. Since our meeting at the mall, she would reach out on occasions. She would share updates or send a text message saying Happy Mothers Day or Merry Christmas. She agreed to attend the party but asked me not to tell Butch because she didn't want him to reach out to Shawn. I agreed to her terms. I didn't tell anyone except my immediate family, not even my daughter. I thought it would be okay because after all, his family knew about Sheila and I thought it would be a good surprise for everyone, in my mind I saw it as a good time to be had by all.

Well…. Shawn, Sheila and Shawn's best friend did make it down to her graduation party. I informed the Disc Jockey that I am waiting on a special guest, so he could quiet the music. She texted me when she arrived, I met her at a side door and they waited to be introduced. The Disc Jockey stopped the music. I told friends and family that I had a "special surprise" for Taí that she had no clue about. Everyone stood up and looked around to see what was happening. I walked them in and Taí screamed and ran toward him and hugged him tightly. Taí was soooo happy. Later that evening, she said mom that was the best gift ever. Taí was glad to walk around and introduce her brother to her friends and family. My family members also greeted and welcomed them.

Butch was in shock, he later told me he was angry with me. He thought I should have told him. (Looking back, yes, I probably should have.) He said it was awkward for him, because he and Sheila did not have a relationship. Butch and Shawn shook hands. The three of them went outside briefly to talk. In hindsight I did not consider how awkward it would be for Butch. In my mind their father-son relationship (or lack thereof) had little to do with my daughter meeting her brother. I also thought Butch's family, his mom, brothers and sister would enjoy seeing him. Unfortunately none of his family came to the party, so Butch later told me it was too much for him to handle on his own.

Later on, Shelia did the same for her son and invited us to attend Shawn's high school graduation party to meet friends and family.

A lot of time had passed, we were just two moms with "only" children, looking out for them. Often times, on some level I thought Sheila got the better deal because she didn't see and go through what we did with Butch. However, I'm sure for Shawn the story may be different.

Besides surprising Tai', I thought it would be a good idea for siblings to get to know each other because the world is small, and I jokingly said I never want her to end up not knowing her brother and dating her brother. As fate would have it, Tai's brother's best friend, the same kid they brought to the graduation party, ended up attending the same college as Tai'. What if Taí and her brother never met and she met him via his best friend, not knowing that was her brother? Taí wondered why her dad didn't have a relationship with Shawn. I told her what I knew but encouraged her to ask her brother and her dad. A few years later, Taí and Butch took a road trip to visit Shawn. Today their contact is minimal, they reach out occasionally on social media. Shawn has children but neither Taí nor Butch have ever met them.

Lesson- We can only choose our friends, not our family.

Chapter 25

～

Dad's Girlfriends

Meeting dad's girlfriends is another touchy subject while co parenting. Women can be emotional as well as unpredictable when it comes to dealing with each other especially when a child is involved. Depending on the age of the child, there are so many factors involved on how to relate to one another. Everyone who likes the father may not like the daughter or the mom. My daughter and I met many women. I would have preferred NOT to on most occasions. Often times Butch was not driving, so whoever he was with at the time would drive him to our home.

Most were on their best behavior, and others not so much. He often received some backlash from his girlfriends because we were on friendly terms. According to my daughter, she didn't like **any** of them, except one and with the others she felt obliged by Butch to be in their presence and be nice to them. If your daughter's father is open to the idea, suggest that their time be one on one. Often times, your daughter may just want to spend time alone with him.

Recognizing each woman has different levels of tolerance and patience, I would offer this; always keep the welfare of your child in mind. As co-parents if you are having a good working relationship, anyone brought into this should respectfully do the same. Try to avoid any situations that may disrespect your child or yourself. Avoid getting into situations that could jeopardize your employment, or your personal freedom. I worked in state government for over thirty years, I've seen many private matters become public quickly over co-parenting miscommunications. As a public employee you may have to report these very private matters to the Internal Affairs Department or to a Public Information Officer. Avoid situations that bring you unrest, and/or disturb your peace. Whenever possible, avoid situations that cause you to have feelings of seriously harming someone. You should take deep breaths, walk around and ask yourself is is worth it? If possible call a reasonable, calm thinking friend, not the one who is putting on her sneakers while you're talking and says I'll pick you up, your too upset to drive. (LoL)

Remove yourself from that space literally and mentally as soon as you can. Usually confrontations are not worth it, and it generally looks different in the morning. Side note, mature adults don't want that heat or that drama around them or their children.

Lesson- Everyone in a relationship with dad, does not necessarily want a relationship with your daughter.

Chapter 26

~

Back On Bae Watch /Dating Tips For Mom

I met my husband when my daughter was almost a year old. I never considered dating anyone I worked with before I met him. I often overheard those male conversations at work and it "scared me straight" about dating coworkers. Was I nervous? The answer is yes. It had been a long time since I dated. My friends and I have worked in the criminal justice system for most of our careers, so we've always had a heightened sense of "caution" while asking okay who's running the background check on Mr. Wonderful. Always be wary of who you let in your space and the space of your children.

Bey and I are both private people, so not many people at work even knew we were dating until we married. However, as I began to spend time with him, I trusted my intuition and sensed that he was safe, he was okay to let in. I never considered him a step-father, in the sense of filling a void. More so of a helpmate and soulmate. He provided us with love, a sense of trust, guidance, and safety for our family.

One example of his kindness was while we were dating, he asked for my house key. When I came home from work, he had cleaned and organized my apartment. I so appreciated that act of kindness. He said, "I saw how overwhelmed you were, I just wanted to help and here's your key back".

While we never sat down and discussed any formal bonus parent do's and don'ts, these are some of the areas that worked for us:

- ❖ Encourage an environment of peace, kindness and respect.

- ❖ Focus on the positive.

- ❖ Try being a bonus parent, not a replacement parent.

- ❖ When things get tough, think through all options first.

A few tips that single moms can follow while dating:

- ✓ Teach him how to value your time. Be with someone who keeps his word.

- ✓ Let him know that your child(ren) will always be a priority.

- ✓ Avoid any drama with the ex.

- ✓ *Listen* intently and ask as many questions as you need to about prior relationships and his children if applicable. File the information in your "*alrighty then* file". This is the mental file we use to store information we gather and which can be retrieved on the dime to mentally fact check any information that gives us pause or seems inconsistent.

✓ Observe if his actions go along with his words, are they consistent? Is he saying one thing, but his actions indicate something different may be going on?

✓ Does he lie about small or insignificant things?

✓ Planning is crucial when you are the pp (primary parent) especially if you have a court-ordered visitation schedule. This must be adhered to, not only for legal reasons but to save you unnecessary aggravation.

✓ Don't push your new "boo" to have a relationship with your child too soon, while your still deciding whether or not he's the "one". Children may attach quickly. You don't want them to become attached and your not sure if he will be in your life. Take your time. Children also need to process the end of the relationship if it doesn't work out.

Lesson-Trust your intuition, your gut is always right.
Don't dismiss your feelings.

Chapter 27

~

All She Needs

A dad is the most important man in his daughter's life. His influence shapes her confidence in herself, her image of herself, and his direct involvement and encouragement will help diminish his daughter's insecurity. A misstep in this bonding can impact her so intensely that all subsequent relationships she has with men are filtered through the lens she has had with her father.

Daughters need their father's unconditional love, support, courage, strength and protection. She needs him. Unlike love, trust and attraction; bonding is something that can be lost, if it's not cultivated. It is cumulative and only gets greater, never smaller.

Bonding develops by:

- ❖ spending time together
- ❖ creating routines
- ❖ making memories

❖ sharing activities

❖ sharing meals together

❖ talking/listening to each other

❖ being involved

Brothers, boyfriends and even husbands can't shape her character the way dad can.

Your influence will be the cornerstone and she will give dad that authority over her life.

Although my daughter is twenty-five, she still questions her wardrobe choices. Saying "my dad would kill me if I wore that".

They share a bond. They share inside jokes, he shares with her, he pushes her to believe she can do anything. She knows that both her dad and my husband are her ride or dies.

As Taí has come into her own while "adulting". She admits her relationship with her dad, influences her choice in men. She admits she has a "type" and it's remarkably similar to the qualities her dad has. She's drawn to young men who are smart, funny, usually a member of a fraternity, smooth talker, emotionally unavailable, with a dose of bad boy.

Lesson-Watch out for the patterns in behaviors, healthy and unhealthy.

Chapter 28

~

Why I Know Dad is Important/ Don't Let Go

My thirty plus years working in the criminal justice system, as well as my training as a mental health professional has given me a frame of reference about human behavior and attachments. A dad or another male caregiver who is present early in your daughter's life, will probably set the model of how a relationship with a man should be.

According to the author, Jennifer Kromberg, Psy.D., dads create a daughter's conscious and unconscious relationship expectations. This has always been in the forefront of my mind and my reason why I try so hard to keep their father-daughter relationship going.

Children don't get to choose their parents. Regardless of the circumstances, children love their parents/caregivers and accept the attachment and love that is given (or is not given). This is important because our patterns of attachment, shape our expectations for future attachments. For a woman this shapes her perception of what is acceptable in a romantic partner.

Within the study of psychology, there is a theory called the Attachment Theory. This concept studied by scholars in the field of developmental psychology (John Bowlby and expanded on by Mary Ainsworth and Hazen & Shaver) were interested in how individuals form an emotional and physical "attachment" to another person. In turn, attempting to describe the dynamics of this interpersonal relationship. As a result of much research, four main styles of attachment have been identified in adults, which begin in how we attach as children:

- secure

- anxious-preoccupied

- dismissive-avoidant

- fearful-avoidant

The premise behind these studies suggest, how children attach in childhood with mom/caregiver can also be found in their adult relationships. For example; if you experienced a *Secure attachment,* you believe and trust that your needs will be met and you have a positive view of yourself and others. You are comfortable with others and don't worry about being alone (meaning for daughter). she has a positive view of herself, her partners and her relationships.

If you experienced an *Anxious attachment,* you may have a negative view of self and a positive view of others, you may be a little insecure. You may want to be close with others, but worry that they don't value you as much as you value them. You may seek high levels of intimacy and approval (meaning for daughter). She may stay around even though he may be wrong for her (fear of abandonment).

If you experienced Dismissive *attachment*, you may desire a higher level of independence, it may appear that you attempt to avoid attaching altogether. May deny the need to be close with others. Subconsciously believing that your needs will not be met. You may avoid others and frame them as untrustworthy (meaning for daughter). She needs constant validation (may push partner away).

If you experienced a *Fearful attachment,* you may experience an unstable view of self and others. You may find it difficult to get close, or to completely trust others (meaning for daughter). Fear of getting close (develop defenses).

Another area to look into for our daughters is trauma. According to journalist, Andrea Bomo, (June 2016) who wrote an article written on Fatherless Daughters, many teenage girls and young women around the world suffer from psychological trauma due to the loss of a father whether it's caused by death, abandonment, divorce, imprisonment, addiction, or emotional absence. This is important because a woman who went through with unhealed dad loss, coupled with dysfunctional behavior will most likely repeat the cycles she experienced in her childhood because her dad was not present. Broken children often grow into broken adults. It can leave an indelible mark on her psyche as she grows into adulthood. Dad's presence fosters and teaches about boundaries and respect and helps put the daughter at ease with other men who they encounter throughout their lives. So, if she didn't grow up with a healthy example, she will have less insight and seek out a man who will replicate the abandonment of her dad.

Parenting is not for punks. I must admit sometimes it scares me, in some situations it has made me fearless and other times it has made me weak in the knees. One thing for sure, parenting is on the job training, no days off. Some days you must be quick on your feet and other days you draw a blank. Each child is different; each child has different behaviors and temperaments.

The blueprint you had growing up is also very important in how you may raise your children.

As a wife, mother, aunt, daughter, and sister, watching and listening to the men in my life has had a profound effect on my growth and development as a woman. My parents were married for over forty years until my father's death in 2008. Growing up I always felt my dad's love and support through his words and his actions. He made me believe I could do and be anything I wanted. He made me feel loved, beautiful and most of all valued.

I now believe because I knew I had that support and love of family, which is why I chose not to stay in the situation with Butch, where I felt hurt and unloved. We live, and we learn.

Admittedly, I can see a few qualities that my dad exhibited, in both Tai's dad and my husband. Ironically I went back to school in my 30's and my husband supported my school endeavor, like my father did for my mom thirty years earlier. Whenever I went somewhere in the community, I felt a sense of pride, people knew I was James Tucker's daughter and Emmett Tuckers' granddaughter. They were regular men in the community but who were well known as well as respected. I was a daddy's girl. Butch told me years later he admired the way my dad took care of me and later our daughter.

The relationship a daughter has or does not have with her father will also affect your parenting toward her. I sometimes felt like I was always picking up the broken pieces, when he would disappoint her. This can present its own challenges. For example, trying to answer questions you have no answer to or telling little white lies to keep dad in a favorable light.

Lesson-Parenting is a privilege, handle with care..

Chapter 29

∾

Nuggets of Wisdom For Our Daughters

_____Pray everyday.

Let your daughter know, she is the valued.

Don't try to convince others to see your worth in their life.

Never dim your light for someone else to shine.

Trust your intuition, you may not see the big picture but if you ask God (or your higher power as

you know them) for clarity/discernment he will surely give it to you.

Protect yourself physically, mentally, and spiritually.

You cannot "fix" someone because you didn't raise them. You can only support them.

When someone shows you who they are, believe them.

Watch a person's actions along with their words.

Be cautious about who you let in your love space and your life space.

Everyone you meet may not be meant to stay in your life.

Don't confuse a lesson for a "life partner".

When considering a long term relationship, look for someone who has similar core-values.

Don't judge others, you never know their backstory.

Happiness is a state of being, not an "arrival point".

Envision what you want, believe you can have it, and put in the necessary work to achieve it.

Lesson-Always tell yourself the truth.

Chapter 30

～

Make A Plan That Works

Surely working together as co-parents is beneficial for everyone. Do the very best you can, when you can.

Successful tips for co-parenting:

✓ Show a willingness to be open and flexible with schedules.

✓ Pick your battles, remember this too shall pass.

✓ Share accomplishments, pictures and grades, as well as discuss change in behavior.

✓ Respect their time with dad.

✓ Recognize that each of you are significant influences in her life.

✓ Practice empathy. Co-parenting is not easy.

Lesson- Children learn what they live.

Conclusion

Looking back, I stick to my original thought. Parenting is tough, co-parenting can be difficult as well. You learn as you go. My hope was to raise a daughter with a sense of independence, confidence and integrity. We tried to build resilience, strength, and character, while trying to set limits and teach values.

There are a few things I would do over, but I would never think of excluding my *hims* (my father, my brother, my daughter's father, and my husband) from this process.

What I can acknowledge is that most of the dads of daughters that I personally know, want to do the right thing. My daughter and her dad continually work on healing the parts of their relationship by making the choices toward acceptance and forgiveness. They ebb and flow and move in the direction they need to at their own pace.

I believe in healing, forgiveness and self-awareness. With self-awareness growth can take place, wrongs can be made right, new learning can take place and broken relationships can take a new shape.

What I know in this co-parenting journey is that children need to feel our love, and support to become their best.

Our village is strong, and for that I am blessed. I am eternally grateful that God entrusted me to be her mother.

Children are our mirrors, as parents what are we reflecting? I once read a quote by Karl Menninger an American Psychiatrist. He said, "What is done to our children, they will do to society".

We all play a part. I hope by sharing my personal journey, you are inspired to give it all you have.

References

Bomo, A. (n.d.). Why we should care about daddyless- fatherless syndrome.

Depression signs and symptoms. (n.d.). Retrieved from webmd

Diamond, J. (n.d.)., Surviving Male Menopause. A Guide for Women and Men (1997) Male Menopause.

Find the Right Therapist. (n.d.). Retrieved from goodtherapy.org

Kromberg, J. (n.d.). How Dads Shape Daughters' Relationships. *Psychology Today*.

Shaven, C. (n.d.). Title Romantic Love Conceptualized as an Attachment Process.

Robert, T. (n.d.). The-9-devastating-effects-of-the-absent-father/, Thurston, Robert.

Raising a Powerful Girl. Body Image & Identity.

www.pbs.org/.../body-image-identity/raising-a-powerful-girl

www.ingramcontent.com/pod-product-compliance
Lightning Source LLC
Chambersburg PA
CBHW021154090426
42740CB00008B/1086

* 9 7 8 0 5 7 8 4 9 3 3 1 2 *